T0000584

First published by PI Kids in 2021.
This library edition published 2023.

Photo credits © 2022 Shutterstock.com
kram9 (seedling, cover); victoriaKh (watermelon slices, back cover); Perutskyi Petro (sprouting seed, pp. 2–3); Thorsten Spoerlein (European nuthatch eating seeds from a flower, p. 5, p. 17); Aitormmfoto (wooden spoons with seeds, p. 6); Natali Zakharova (watermelon seeds, p. 6); StudioPhotoDFlorez (creative fruit layout, p. 7); Lotus Images (orchid, p. 8); Dionisvera (poppyhead, p. 9); Palokha Tetiana (three ripe coconuts, p. 9); amenic181 (green sprout in soil, p. 10); YewLoon Lam (young lotus seed, p. 10); Yellow Cat (pumpkin seeds, p. 11); Artography (half peeled broad bean, p. 11); showcake (underground root view of stages of growing plants, pp. 12–13); Aleksandr Stennikov (watermelon slice, p. 14); Billion Photos (dandelion blowing seeds, p. 14); OlegD (coconut on the beach, p. 15); Phagalley (dog with seeds stuck in the fur, p. 16); Songquan Deng (cherry blossom tree, p. 18); Stephen Moehle (Redwood National and State Parks, California, p. 19); Rawpixel.com (cupping plants with hands, p. 20); New Africa (kids and volunteers planting trees, p. 21); Alexey U (dandelion blowing seeds, pp. 22–23)

Customer Service: 1-877-277-9441 or customerservice@phoenixinternational.com

Published by PI Kids, an imprint of Phoenix International Publications, Inc.

8501 West Higgins Road
Chicago, Illinois 60631

34 Seymour Street
London W1H 7JE

Heimhuder Straße 81
20148 Hamburg

PI Kids is a trademark of Phoenix International Publications, Inc., and is registered in the United States.

www.pikidsmedia.com

Library of Congress Control Number: 2022920542

ISBN: 979-8-7654-0161-3

Plant a Seed

An imprint of Phoenix International Publications, Inc.
Chicago • London • New York • Hamburg • Mexico City • Sydney

How SEEDS FORM

Most plants begin life as seeds.

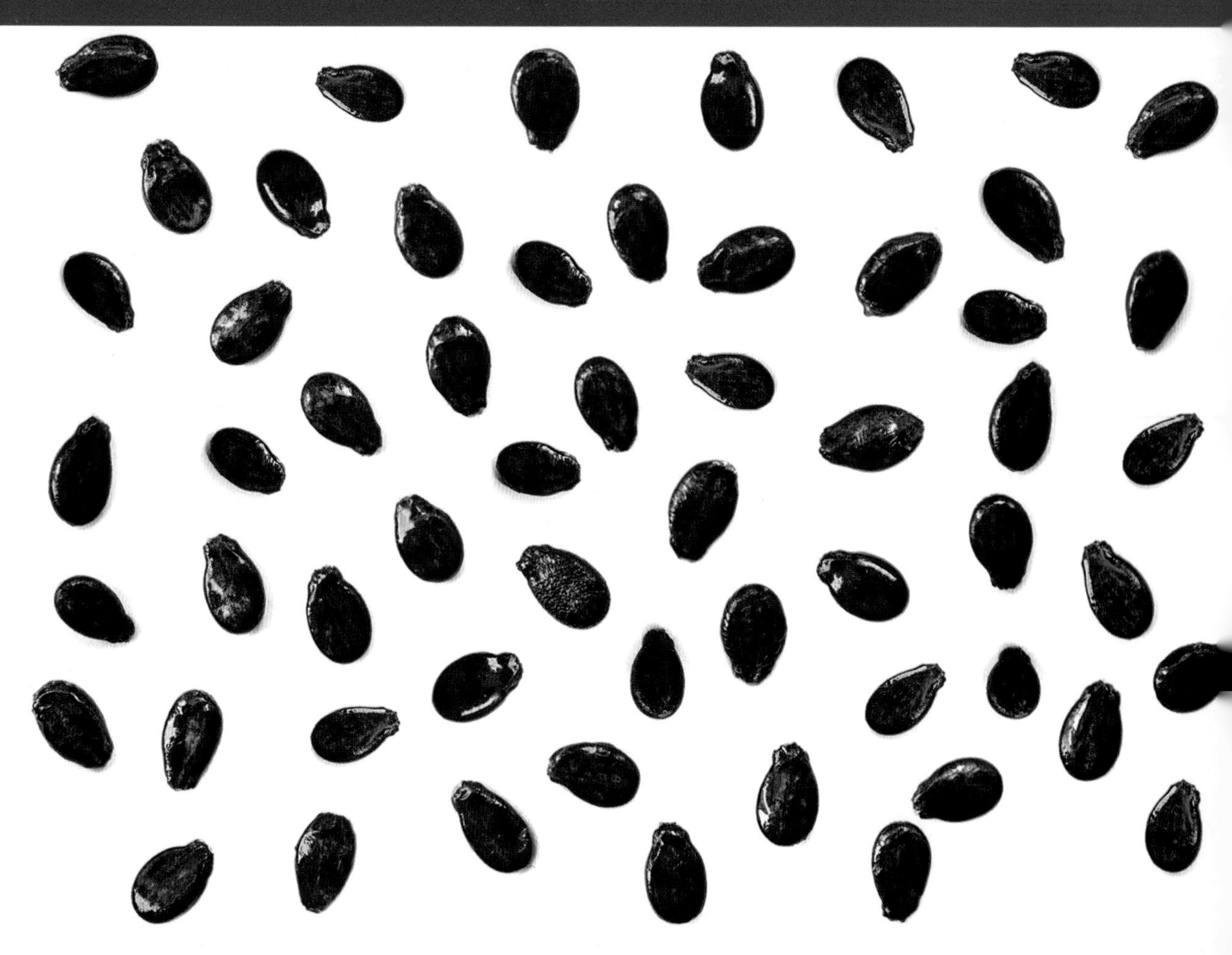

Seeds need air, water, the right temperature, healthy soil, and the right amount of light to grow into new plants.

When plants grow, they form new seeds inside flowers or cones. In flowering plants, a fruit often holds the seeds.

Seeds come in **different sizes.**

Orchid seeds are **as small as dust particles.**

The **seed pod** of a poppy contains many small seeds.

The **coconut is one of the largest seeds** in the plant kingdom!

How SEEDS GROW

A seed contains a miniature plant, called an embryo, that can develop into a full-grown plant.

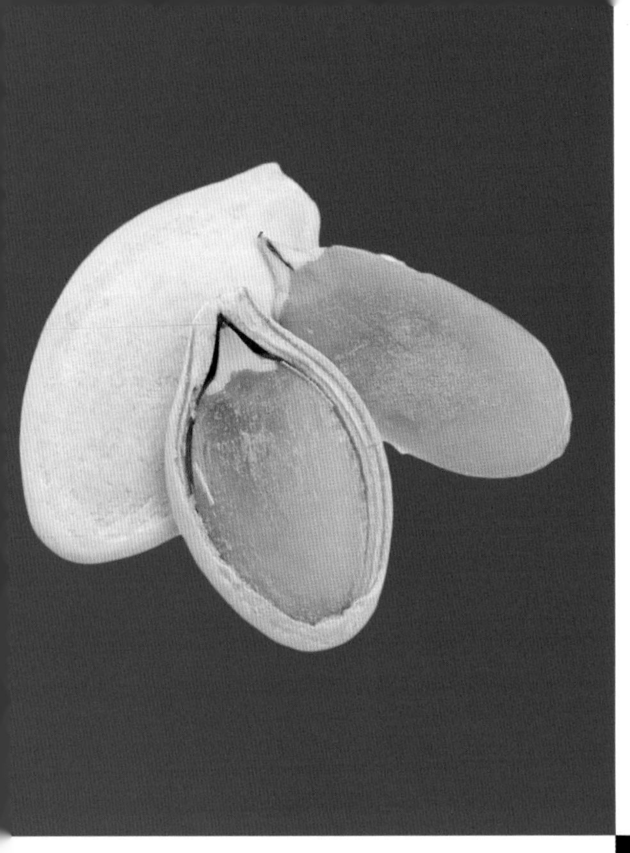

The outer shell of a seed, called a seed coat, protects the embryo.

Inside the seed, a nutritious material provides food to the embryo.

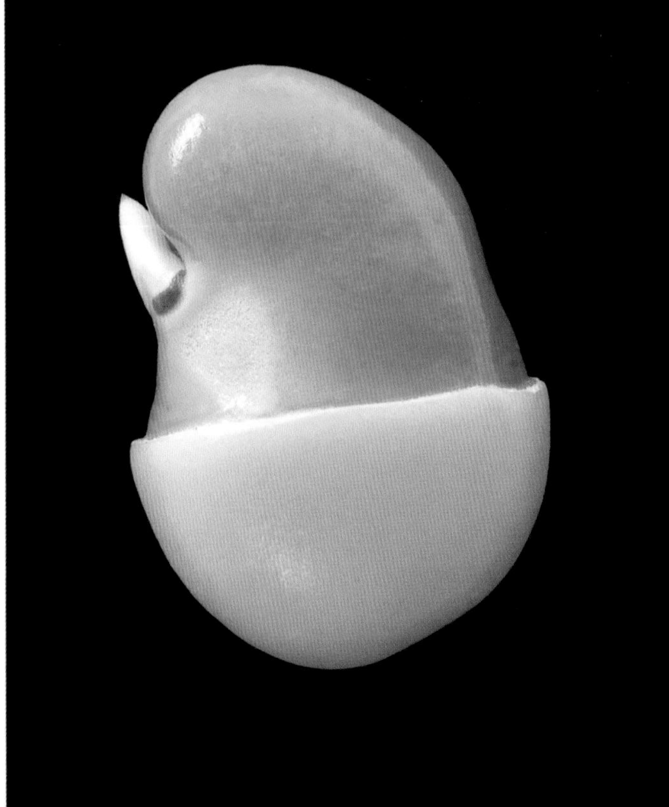

When a seed starts to grow, parts of the embryo break out of the seed coat.

One part grows downward. It becomes the plant's roots, which take in water and food from the soil.

Other parts grow upward. They become the plant's stem and leaves, which take in sunlight.

How SEEDS TRAVEL

Some plants have fruits or pods that **burst open to scatter** the seeds inside.

Some seeds, such as dandelion seeds, have fluffy parts that help them **drift through the air**.

Some plants, such as coconut palms, drop their seeds in nearby water. These seeds have waterproof coverings that let them float far away.

Animals carry seeds to other places. Seeds with sticky or prickly seed coats stick in the fur of animals. The seeds drop to the ground later.

When birds and other animals eat seeds, the **seeds pass through their bodies** and often end up far from where they ate them.

Most seed-bearing trees grow their seeds in fruits or pods. They are known as flowering trees.

Trees are the **largest and oldest living things on Earth**. Some trees live for hundreds or even thousands of years!

PLANT A TREE!

Arbor Day is a holiday observed in many countries by planting trees.

The first Arbor Day celebration was held in the state of Nebraska in the United States on April 10, 1872. More than one million trees were planted!